MW00948194

THᴇ
OPEN YOUR
PRACTICE
BLUEPRINT

The Business of Therapy, Made Simple™

By Laura Gransberry, MA, LMFT, and Dustin Gransberry, HC

Table of Contents

Introduction

Let's start at the very beginning. You have likely ordered a copy of this book because you are feeling stuck or scared about opening a private practice, or you want to be as informed as possible before taking that leap and committing to act on your dreams.

We are so excited you have taken this step, and truly believe this Blueprint, and our Master Course, are going to get you there with some great insight, resources, and hopefully a few laughs along the way.

The three biggest problems we've heard from counselors, therapists, psychologists, and social workers wanting to open private practice are:

1. They can't decide where to begin
2. They aren't sure how to put the pieces together
3. They can't stay motivated

We're here to share The Open Your Practice Blueprint to help you get unstuck so you know what to do to move forward!

As we sit here on our couch writing, our newborn son sleeping soundly in the other room, I can't help but reflect on how far we have come on this journey. I remember when all three of the problems listed above plagued me everyday. I felt completely overwhelmed and stuck.

And now here we are teaching others how to solve these problems in what we believe to be the most efficient and simple way possible. It's pretty remarkable what happens when you set your mind on fixing a process this complex. There are so many ins-and-outs to this process, no wonder so many people simply choose to stay where they are. You don't need to put your dreams on hold, and settle for the status quo.

The Open Your Practice Blueprint has tremendous stand-alone value, and it works in conjunction with the more in-depth Open Your Practice Master Course. The Blueprint is the *what* to do, and the Master Course is the *how* to do it.

We wanted to make this Blueprint, and the therapy business startup checklist you'll find in it, as accessible as possible because it is truly what I was so desperate for when I set out on this journey. I just wanted some direction. Give me a list, and I'll start checking things off! But the list I was looking for didn't exist. Until now!

You can get started in private practice with the Blueprint. However, if you would like to go deeper and really understand how to quickly succeed in private practice, how to build a business structure that runs as efficiently as possible, the OYP Master Course is for you. To get your copy email us at info@openyourpractice.com for more information. Or visit www.openyourpractice.com.

We are so excited to go on this journey with you. Take some time and enjoy these few pages, and we'll see you on the other side!

Laura's Story

I was 13 years old when I realized I wanted to be a therapist. I was always curious about other people, what made them tick and how and why they did the things they did.

I had been to some therapy myself for being significantly bullied in my elementary school years. I saw what it was all about, and I decided that I wanted to help people, as I had been helped.

So I sat down with my parents when I was 13 years old and told them that being a therapist is what I wanted to do. They didn't even bat an eye- they said, "That's great! We'll support you in every way that we can." I never looked back.

The first part of my life was spent in LA. When I was 13, my family moved to a small town in Santa Barbara County where I grew up and finished high school. I couldn't wait to get to college.

For my undergraduate work I majored in psychology at UCSB. It wasn't an easy road. The psychology major was impacted, which meant I needed a 3.5 GPA for admission to the major and I was .05 below. Would I not be able to pursue my dream?

Being tenths of a grade point away from my dream felt terrible. I was frustrated, but I did not lose hope. I battled through bureaucracy, spending 6 months and an entire summer in the appeals process.

I ended up in the university dean's office because I had exhausted every avenue of appeal to be admitted into the major. I explained that this wasn't just about psychology undergrad for me, this was about my whole career.

I had been advised by other administrative staff to switch majors to communications, or something else that was not impacted by a strict GPA requirement. I thought that was simply preposterous. That was not going to work for me. Not only would I have had to take two more quarters worth of classes and incur the tuition expense, it wouldn't move me in the direction of my dreams.

I told the dean the story of my appeals process, explaining every hoop I had already jumped through, and how this decision would impact my career and life. He understood my determination. My conviction to pursue a career as a therapist in private practice won him over and within 24 hours I had a letter in my hands, welcoming me to the psychology department!

This experience taught me two very important life lessons:

> 1) Don't ever give up on something that is important to you. Don't ever quit pursuing something that sets your heart on fire.

> 2) If you are going to commit to something, go all in. If you aren't going to put your all into it, don't do it at all. Do it with every fiber of your being.

These lessons have become such a core facet of my personality. I'm driven, sometimes to a fault, to do the best I can in nearly every circumstance. If I take something on, I'm all in. I don't leisure in the pursuit. My passions in life are never a secret. I wear them on my sleeve. I don't know how to operate any other way.

After graduation, I knew that I needed to go to graduate school. There was an Antioch University locally in Santa Barbara. I applied over the summer for fall admission, and was accepted.

Santa Barbara isn't really a town you stay in after graduation. Most of my friends had moved away after college, and at that time in my life I felt a calling to see more of the world. One quarter into grad school, I took a trip to visit a friend in Seattle and decided that I wanted to move there.

I transferred to the Antioch University Seattle campus the following quarter, and moved my entire life up north to a city where I only knew a couple of people. During graduate school I completed a dual internship in community mental health as well as at a residential eating disorder facility.

I worked my tail off pulling 60-70 hour weeks, holding a full time job, taking classes, in addition to the dual internship. After graduating from my masters degree program, I continued working as floor staff for the summer.

In that role, I ran groups, supported therapeutic meals, and managed crisis when necessary (which was often). Though taxing, it was actually a welcome break from the 70-hour-a-week-hell I had put myself through, holding down a job while in school.

That summer after graduation was awesome. I remember spending most weekends at the beach soaking up the sun and learning how to paddle board. As the summer came to a close, and I accepted a full time position at the residential eating disorder facility as a primary therapist.

In total, I spent five years with that company collecting a significant amount of experience and building a strong community. It wasn't all roses though. The work was absolutely exhausting due to the elevated level of care that was required. It was emotionally intensive and draining to the point that some days after work I couldn't function.

I knew that there had to be more to life. I knew that the goal of going to graduate school was to someday have a private practice. How could I get there?

As it happened, I went to work for another agency for awhile. I collected more good experience, but was getting no closer to my dream of private practice.

By this time I had a little over seven years of residential eating disorder treatment experience under my belt. I was good at my job, and at times the work was immensely rewarding. Seeing a teenager reclaim their life and learn to love themselves again was amazing. It was an honor to be a part of their journey.

The problem was that it came at a heavy cost for me emotionally. I came home completely drained of all energy, giving the work all I had. And the worst part? I was actually going backwards financially. Thanks to income based repayments, and a salary that was barely enough for me to live on, I was no closer to paying off my student loans. They were getting bigger.

I was treading water in every aspect of my life. But then I met this guy who had a really incredible story...

Dustin's Story

One of my earliest memories is ringing the doorbell of a neighbor, standing on the front stoop waiting for her to answer the door with a mail order catalog in my hands.

My Dad had showed me that with this mail order company, if I sold enough cookies, candles, and whatever else was in their book I could get a new bike *and* a Nintendo Entertainment System.

Growing up, there was never enough money for the things that I wanted. So I began door to door sales at age 5.

I am a product of my family of origin. My Dad inspired my love of sales and entrepreneurship, and my Mother's influence drew me to coaching.

My Mom called me her sweet boy. I'd always been drawn to helping people. I began coaching wrestling in the 8th grade and continued through college. In High School, I was that guy that people sat with and told their problems. I pictured my life as a therapist.

In my mind, I looked something like Freud. I had white hair and a white goatee, and a big black leather chair that I would sit in and listen to people tell me their problems. And I would help them. So it was off to the University of Oregon to study psychology on my road to open a private practice. But it was not to be.

The High School teachers had all told me to go to college, so that I could get a good job. But I saw them struggling financially, and I found it impossible to take their advice for me seriously because I did not want to be poor.

Then one day close to graduation I found myself at a network marketing meeting where people were talking about helping people by showing them how to go into business for themselves and getting wealthy at the same time. Was it too good to be true? I didn't know but I had to find out for myself.

I delayed going to college for a few years to pursue two business ventures: a coffee servicing company (I am from Seattle after all) and the network marketing idea that had captured my curiosity.

I spent thousands of hours listening to motivational and inspirational presentations hoping to find the secret of success. I had two giant suitcases full of audio tapes from business leaders telling their stories and advice. When I wasn't listening to a tape I was reading a book on self-help or personal development. I go all in on things.

Eventually I got FOMO. My friends were off having the time of their lives in college, and I was working 80-90 hour weeks consistently, with no real end in sight. I sold out of my business interests and decided to go to school at Tulane University in New Orleans.

I studied business at Tulane. Then Hurricane Katrina swept through the gulf, broke the levees, flooded the city, and put the area under quarantine.

Next stop Pittsburgh PA, attending Carnegie Mellon University, to study entrepreneurship while NOLA dried out. After a winter semester in the frozen north I welcomed a chance to get back south to warmer weather and help with the rebuilding efforts of my adopted home.

After Tulane graduation I moved to Tucson, Arizona and took a job in international logistics. Then I moved back to Seattle because I wanted to build buildings. The draw I felt was incredible, much like wanting to go to Tulane. I would not be denied, but I had no idea how to make it happen. I willed it so.

I enrolled in the University of Washington's construction management program, and I found work on a large project where I applied as a general laborer. I was hired and then put in charge of a team of carpenters. This was cool, except I didn't have a clue what I was doing.

I spent every night in the library reading every book I could find on carpentry. Did you know that wood has different names depending on how long you cut it and where you put it? What the heck is a sixteen-penny?

Before the project ended I'd been promoted to assistant superintendent. But then a super crazy thing began to happen. The bottom fell out of the economy. And everyday I watched newscasters lie about why the financial collapse was happening.

I knew better than to believe what I was being told. But I didn't know what the truth was, so as I had done many times before I began to dig deep to find out.

Short answer: there are, in fact, quite a few nasty things which are kept secret from the public. These things are upsetting to learn about.

I dug deeper and found myself tumbling down a rabbit-hole of Internet and library research which led me to a dark emotional place. I asked myself, 'If there is this much negative information hidden from the public, and the universe is in balance, then doesn't there have to be as much positive information that is kept hidden as well...?'

I climbed out of the conspiracy tailspin by focusing on all of the incredible, lesser known discoveries in health sciences and nutrition. I discovered Max Gerson, Wilhelm Reich, Ann Wigmore, Weston Price, Francis Pottenger, T. Colin Campbell, Royal Raymond Rife, and Joshua Rosenthall.

There is a great scene from the 1991 movie Hook starring Robin Williams and Dustin Hoffman, my namesake, where Williams playing an older, fatter, Peter Pan remembers why he left Neverland to find his happy place. (He wanted to be a father).

I wanted to be a Health Coach and share all that I had learned about holistic health, healing, personal empowerment, and entrepreneurship. I enrolled at the Institute for Integrative Nutrition in New York. After completion, I received my board certification through the American Association of Drugless Practitioners and opened a private practice as a Health Coach.

I leased an office with my name on the door along with a chiropractor, acupuncturist, and two massage practitioners. I built my health coaching private practice from the ground up, facing many of the same challenges therapists face when building their practices.

I worked tirelessly to build a marketing plan, and I still get calls even today based on the marketing work I set in motion years ago.

Over time, my practice evolved from a focus on health coaching to business coaching, which is what I was doing when I met Laura.

I saw how much she was struggling with her job. Since I had built a private practice already I knew for certain it was not only possible, but that she would definitely be successful.

We discussed her fears extensively. I could see how much she wanted to pursue her dreams, but I had empathy for how stuck she felt.

We embraced the challenge together, took massive action, documented what worked and what didn't, and now she runs a successful private practice in Seattle.

We knew we could save clinicians valuable time, money, and stress if we shared what we had learned through our struggles. We decided it simply wasn't an option to let this process be so inefficient any longer.

Laura and I have partnered to build Open Your Practice to share the secrets of building and succeeding in private practices from scratch, with the least amount of time and money necessary, to help you achieve the most amount of joy and freedom from the work.

The Open Your Practice Master Course began as a live event and was exceptionally well received, but we were asked over and over to 1) make it available nationally and 2) create a way for therapists, social workers, coaches, and counselors to study it at their own pace.

We're excited to tell you: now you can, because The Open Your Practice Master Course is available online.

Dustin asks Laura some important questions to give you guidance about the private practice start-up journey...

Doubts, Fears & Motivation

Why did you continue pursuing agency work when private practice was your dream?

Fear. Which sometimes can be a good motivator. But it kept me bound. I was definitely bound to that paycheck that came in every two weeks. I wasn't getting paid a lot for the amount of effort that I was putting in, which is a big complaint of people in this line of work- it's often just enough to survive, maybe not even that.

So the idea of quitting, and then private practice startup seemed like a Grand Canyon leap. I kept going around in my head with thoughts like, "How do I pay bills in the meantime?" "How can I cover my student loan in the meantime?" "How can I do this when I'm just getting by as it is?" The build time seemed impossible. I reasoned with myself that I would be making zero dollars for an uncertain amount of time, and it seems no one can even really tell me what that amount of time is...It just seemed impossible.

To cope, I just put my head down and kept working. I kept going back to my job for the next installment of the paycheck, even though it wasn't enough. I didn't know how to bridge that gap. I didn't know how to make that happen for me. I was single and just trying to make it in a growing city with a high cost of living. It was just another hurdle. I was able to look back and see that there was significant adversity on my journey to the professional counseling arts. There was adversity when I was 13 and bullied. There was adversity when I was in undergrad. There was adversity when I was in graduate school and I transferred from one state to another. There had been adversity for me every step of the way on this path.

What motivated you to stay committed to the therapy profession?
I love helping other people. There is something incredibly rewarding when you see your work come to fruition. When you see someone really grasp onto a concept you've been working on together. When you clients really start to embrace their recovery. When a family system finds a more functional way of operating. When they find better self-esteem and you've walked with them on that journey, you know how far they've come and the work they've put in, that's super rewarding to me.

I really like the idea of helping people find themselves. I love helping people become their best self. That's what kept me motivated. I also developed a passion for teaching. I teach at the masters degree program that I graduated from Antioch University Seattle, and I help students figure out how to be a great clinician.

When I was in grad school, I once had a supervisor ask me how I wanted to shape my art. I have always hung onto that question, and it drives much of the teaching of my students today. I am very focused on the art of therapy and what it looks like to shape your art. I love helping students cultivate their art. Surely there is science involved in our profession, but I love talking about the art that exists as well. There is so much potential there.

Did you make constant and steady progress towards your goals?

My journey to private practice has not been one quantum leap after another. Many times it felt sedentary, like I was making no progress at all. I had actually attempted to start private practice immediately after graduating from graduate school. I was an LMFTA, so I couldn't take insurance, we were in the middle of a recession, and I didn't get it off the ground. I was trying to work a job and launch private practice at the same time. And it just failed really quickly because I didn't have a path. I didn't have a guide. I didn't know what I was doing.

It was a frustrating thing to feel like I gave it a shot and had failed. I wasn't unhappy though. I had a job. It was paying me money. I worked with good people. There were things to be grateful for, and I didn't always feel like I was backsliding but I certainly didn't feel like I was moving forward.

How did you deal with and overcome all those fears?

There was really a tipping point where the amount of stress and exertion that my job was costing me no longer outweighed my fear. I reached an "even though I'm scared I'm going to do it anyway" kind of mentality. I also had you (my then adoring fiancé, now turned adoring husband) there to be the cheerleader I needed. To tell me I could do it, and that it was going to be successful.

You had built a successful practice already, so you knew not only that it could be done, but that I could absolutely do it. I talk to my clients and my students a ton about tipping points. I think it's such a core component of our psychology as humans. You can find a tipping point for almost anything. When something just becomes too much...tipping point. When you are so motivated you just can't stop running in that direction...tipping point. Really anything that moves you to change in any direction...tipping point. For me, the struggle finally bested the fear. Tipping point.

If you could talk to yourself back when you first graduated from your masters degree program, and could give yourself some advice, what would that be? Would you wait those seven years?
No! I wouldn't wait seven years. There's a lot of people that do agency work to get their supervision hours, and I think that makes sense to me. If you are at a place where you don't have to pay for supervision, and it's included, then that's part of your salary. There can be a real benefit to that. But if someone told me that I could start private practice right out of the gate, and that it was going to be successful, and I was guaranteed that, then I wouldn't have hesitated.

The hindsight is 20/20. I would have known I would be ok, and I would have paid an outside source for supervision. I would be guaranteed that I could make enough money to cover the supervision cost. To carry the business costs. I wouldn't have felt so scared. So "don't wait as long" would be my advice to my graduate school self. And especially if I had a guide, then definitely don't wait as long.

Dealing with Imposter Syndrome

Did you ever experience any amount of imposter syndrome?

Yes, I experienced that. I still do in a lot of areas. As I write this I am wondering if I am good enough to be self-publishing a book. Me? An author? I've always wanted that...but do I really know what I'm talking about? Yes. I do. But the thoughts are still there. I still battle them. When you are a really young therapist, there's this moment of "why are these people coming to see me? I have no idea what I am doing." But there's no way around that.

You're going to be young and green for awhile. And you do know what you are doing. You went to school. You had training. You completed your internship. You are new at this, yes, but give yourself some grace! You can't know everything there is to know right out of the gate. Trust me. I've tried.

When I was wrapping up my internship at the residential eating disorder facility, I was sitting in one of my final supervision sessions with one of my favorite supervisors. He's the one that talked to me about shaping my art. Gold, that man was (and probably still is). Pure gold. He said to me that someone started at our facility some time back and told him that they wanted to know everything there was to know about working with this population so they could do everything right.

Knowing that this was ridiculous and completely impossible after everything I had learned in my internship, I started laughing and with a smirk on my face I said, "Who said that?!?!"

He smiled and said, "YOU!" I was mortified. I couldn't believe I had thought you could learn everything so quickly and do everything "right." That just doesn't exist in the therapy world. It won't with your clients, and it won't with building your practice either. Grace is the answer here, friends. Grace with yourself when learning something new is always the answer.

You will have several moments of "I don't know if I'm going to be good enough. Am I good enough to start a private practice? Am I good enough to have clients refer to me? Will other clinicians refer to me?"

The majority of new client marketing in this profession is word of mouth. Especially in the beginning, self doubt will be ever present. So yes, I had all of those thoughts and fears, but the answer was also yes, people will refer to me and I will be just fine.

What advice do you have about imposter syndrome regarding private practice?
There's anxiety and fear when starting a business in any situation. My advice is: Don't suffer in isolation. Talk to someone about it. The chances that someone else feels that way, or has felt that way are pretty high.

We advocate heavily in our course about having a community to talk to, having a mentor, having someone there to be your cheerleader. I believe it's crucial. Most people want to be cheerleaders for people that they know are good humans and going to do great in life. So just stepping in to that vulnerability and saying "I'm scared of this, and I don't know if I actually should be doing this, am I going to be good at it?" Just saying it out loud takes so much of the fear's power away.

Is that what you did? Admitting your fears out loud?
Yes. Them, lean into those around you. They will be there for you and prop you up. But you have to take that first step and say the words. Make yourself vulnerable, and you will grow. I promise.

Professional Development

Did you have enough help? Did you know enough?
I had well meaning people tell me what they thought I
should do, unfortunately much of what I heard was
contradictory. Someone helped me get a business
license online, but beyond that I was lost as to what to
do to make the practice successful. I didn't know
marketing. I didn't know what kind of tools and
resources I needed to run my business efficiently and
effectively.

There were all kinds of missing pieces. Huge, gaping
holes. Looking back, I realize that if I had known those
things, if I had a blueprint to follow I could have
gotten my practice off the ground. I could have built
it up to be successful, but there were roadblocks in my
efforts because I was uninformed about the right
course of action.

The most frustrating part of this was how often people
would tell me, "It depends." I asked a lot of clinicians
about build time, and what about this, and what
about that, and how do you brand it, and invariably
the answer came back, "well I don't know" or "It
depends!" (exasperated sigh emoji). No one could
give me a concrete answer. And so I just felt that I was
caught in the waves being sloshed around. It was
tough.

If I had stayed at it, with those gaps in understanding,
without the blueprint that I now have I don't think I
would have built my practice the way that I wanted it.
It certainly wouldn't be as efficient as the one I have
now, I'll tell you that much! I was doing everything in
paper! Now we have digital practice management

systems, and procedures for all the time consuming elements, which we talk about at length in our course. If my practice had gotten off the ground, I'm sure it would have been fine, but it would not have been what I would have wanted it to be. What I knew it could be.

This is why we have had several former (and current) private practice owners come to our live event workshops, and that totally makes sense to me. They wanted to fill in the gaps and holes they had in their businesses which they were totally unaware of when they started. They were looking for ways to run a more fun and efficient therapy business. Isn't that the whole point of this endeavor? To do help people, do fulfilling work, and enjoy your life? That's the whole reason we built the Open Your Practice Master Course.

I know first hand how inefficient the business launch process is. I know what it feels like to start and fail. I know what it looks like to have big missing pieces once you have started. The whole thing is cumbersome, and muddy, and frustrating. We set out to fix all that. I couldn't stand the idea that good clinicians were being kept from their best work, and their best schedule, and their best lives because of the confusion and fear. I knew we had to fix it.

The silver lining here is that there is a secondary impact for our clients. The more great clinicians we have in private practice, the more resources are available for those in need. We need clinicians in private practice to do the hard work: To do the tele-health so that clients in underserved areas can receive the care they need. To take the tough cases.

To care for others, while also caring for themselves and living a well balanced life.

How does professional development play a role in the process of opening a private practice?
There is already a minimum requirement in terms of professional development in our field, which takes the form of continuing education credits. But we are both proponents of going above and beyond that. Personal development can be anything from a motivational speaker's book that I'll pick up and read, or simply making sure that I am staying on top of my self care, which is a huge part of this field and this process.

Like most people that go into this line of work, I am not satisfied with being stationary. I like to grow. I like to better myself. I believe that it serves our clients when we continue to work on ourselves, both personally and professionally. There's an element where we like to help other people, but we also have a strong connection to who we are. (At least I hope this is the case!) I often find myself saying something to my client and thinking, "Oh man, that's a growth edge for me as well. That's something I should work on myself or explore in my own life." I like to practice what I preach. I think it would be pretty hypocritical to want to run a business to help others change if you were not willing to invest in change for yourself. I think most social workers, coaches, and therapists are like-minded in that way.

What did you wish you had known about this career when you were in undergrad?
I wish I had known how many possibilities are in this profession. The type of work you can do, how you

build your practice, etc. When I was young, I had a pretty traditional perspective (from movies and TV) on what therapy looked like: you know, the office with the chair...which is ironically actually what I ended up doing.

However, there are a lot of things that you can do and pursue with these credentials. Writing, for instance, and teaching, and education. I see a lot of highly specialized therapy practices with what we do now. One of the most fantastic is equine therapy, where you integrate the use of horses for therapy. I love horses. There is something truly magical about them in my mind. I feel this way about dogs too. These animals have an immense capacity for empathy and love. The therapeutic indications are incredible. I've seen some amazing breakthroughs for people as a result of working with animals.

In undergrad I wasn't aware of this depth, these different parts of our field. It was all studies about cognition, behavioral responses, Pavlov, Stanford and their prison experiment, and on, and on, and on. Valuable: yes. Necessary as a foundation: of course. But dry, narrow, and lacking art: most definitely.

What did you wish you knew had known about this career when you were still in grad school?
I wish I had known all of the things that this Blueprint and the corresponding Open Your Practice Master Course deliver. The biggest struggle for me about grad school was that the business side of therapy is not taught. That's why we created this company and all of our products.

I hear from colleague after colleague, and I hear from student after student when they were in school that this was, and still is, such a huge missing piece. The business mindset is not something that comes naturally to us. We are therapy people. Our brains work in a language of empathy, emotions, patterns, behavior, compassion, care, and concern. It typically does not work in numbers, cash flow, revenue, taxes, licenses, and marketing. It's a lot of work to turn something complex into something simple and easy to understand. It's taken a tremendous amount of effort for us to turn the muddiness and cloudiness of this process into a clear blueprint that you can follow.

There is a lot to be learned there, and I wish I had known this information in graduate school before I needed it to open my practice, so I could plan my moves ahead. And that is precisely what we have created. That is precisely what the Master Course offers. It simplifies this process in a way to optimize efficiency, saving you immense time, money, and headache. We've put it into a language that is easier to understand, and I'm really proud of that. We set out to solve this for people. To remove this barrier so the fear is less obstructive.

We offer the checklist here, and it's a great place to start, but the class is the real meat and potatoes of the journey. The resources alone are worth the investment. We tell you exactly what you will need, and where to get it. It's exactly what I wanted and didn't have when I was building.

Is Private Practice Is Right for Me?

When did you know for sure that private practice was right for you?

I decided in my teenage years to become a therapist, and the goal was still the same when I was in grad school. It was always the goal. For me, it was a matter of how. I knew that what I wanted was a private practice because that's where I could do my best work, and the work that I wanted to do. It was never a question of if for me, it was a question of how. I just didn't know how to bridge the gap. I wanted to be in private practice because I wanted more freedom. I wanted to be able to grow a family and to be able to be there for them, in other words, in control of my schedule.

My experience growing up was that my parents were very present. They both worked and I was an after-school daycare-kid, which was fine, but they were always there. When I was in high school they were always at all of my sporting events. I played every sport imaginable before settling into a year round volleyball schedule, and they were present every step of the way. I remember my dad driving me 40 minutes each way tot club practice in Santa Barbara 2 to 3 days a week, and countless tournaments on weekends. They certainly could have chosen other things to do, but they were ever present for both my sister and me.

As a result, I wanted the flexibility in my schedule to be there for my children's activities as well. I wanted to be able to say that I wasn't going to see clients on Friday evenings because my son had such and such event, and I'm going to be there. I wanted to decide how I spent my time. I wanted the ability to earn more money without having to ask a boss for a raise - paying off student loans was a motivating factor.

Private practice felt like the best, or the only way to accomplish those things that I wanted after looking at other jobs and seeing how they were structured. I saw a pattern in how jobs wanted you to work 8 hours a day, 40 hours a week, to commute in traffic, show up at their location, earn a pittance in exchange for a huge amount of effort, all so you can pay too much in taxes, relax on the weekend, and do it all over again the next week. No thanks!

Do you want the flexibility to work different hours on different days to accommodate the things you want to do in life that are not working? Well, too bad if you have a job. Want the option to take Fridays off (and get paid the same)? Not an option in the job world.

I saw that people around me accepted this status quo exchange but it always grated against me. Private practice seemed to me like the only way to get those things in life that I wanted, and I could see that I would not get them from a traditional job. I don't fault them, but agencies demand a lot from you in terms of your time and effort, for little money. Let's look at this objectively: Agencies are businesses, right? They want to optimize their bottom line by getting the most out of you for the least amount of money they can afford to pay for the job you do. I know this isn't something that a lot of people like to talk about, but it's the truth.

I don't want to speak poorly about any of my former employers. I don't believe they did anything out of the ordinary. It seems unreasonable to blame them for the fact that they want the most out of their employees for the least amount of money. I realized however, that I was tired of building their bottom line. I wanted to build my own.

The most frustrating part of wanting to start private practice was not having a guide. Every time I turned to anyone for advice and guidance it was met with the non-committal: "maybe" or "it depends." ON WHAT??? What are those levers, so I know which ones to pull? So I can plan! No one could tell me. There was nothing concrete. I was part of some Facebook groups where people would ask questions and the responses would come back in an array of possibilities. How helpful is that really when the answers you get back are contradictory? 5 people like this headshot, and another 5 like that one. How are you supposed to know the right path with that type of advice? I was looking for someone to come in and say, "I did this...and it was successful. This is what you do." I was looking for an action plan. Not just an, "I'm not sure, maybe, it depends," plan.

I did get good advice from select sources along the way, which we talk about in the Open Your Practice Master Course. Like how beneficial it is to have your office close to home. It's truly been a blessing to be so close to home. I would have benefited greatly from a curriculum, much like we get in school. It seems so simple to me when I think about it, I ask myself, "why didn't this exist?" And the answer that comes back is: It has been a massive amount of work to collect, validate, simplify, and teach the business side of therapy. Years of work went into developing the Open Your Practice Blueprint and Open Your Practice

Master Course, and it is our hope that it will propel you like a slingshot to your goals, saving you massive amounts of time, energy, mistakes, and money.

I could see that there were a lot of people in private practice and they looked to me like they were successful, but for the life of me I couldn't figure out how they did it, or more specifically what steps they took. The gap was still so vast. How do I pay for stuff in the meantime? It literally felt like trying to leap over the Grand Canyon. That was so frustrating to me because I could see what I wanted on the other side. I could see all the benefits that came with it. I just couldn't see how to get there.

Why would you recommend private practice?
I would recommend private practice to people who want to have more ownership over their time and income, and want control over the type of people they see in their practice. When you are working for an agency you see clients that the agency chooses for you. You don't get to choose. In private practice you decide. I know clinicians that only see couples. They are strictly couples counselors. They don't see families, they don't see individuals, and they never plan to. And if that's your goal, say you've poured all that money into getting Gottman certified and you just want to be a couple's counselor, that means private practice for you.

There's a lot more choice and control in private practice. You get to pull the levers that control your business. You pull the lever of setting your cash rate, in other words you determine what your hour is worth to see private pay clients. You pull the lever of what you set your hours at; you determine when you work and when you don't. You pull the lever of how many clients you are willing to see in a week, what your billable hours will be. You get to design all of that. You get to optimize all of those things for your life in private practice. In agency work, with a job, you don't get to determine those things, your life is on someone else's schedule.

Who is right for private practice? Is there a certain type of personality or person that should not go into private practice?
If you have a tendency to be timid or to second guess yourself, make sure you thicken that skin a bit first. This guide should take a lot of the guesswork out. However, if you are one of those people that are really reliant on the comfort of a paycheck coming in every two weeks, and you really couldn't dream of that not happening, then I would think long and hard about going into private practice.

Business ownership comes with a variable income. Some months your business makes more than others. You can generally get a baseline of what an average monthly income will look like once you have been in private practice for a while. But there is always going to be variations in your business income (gross revenue) due to cancellations and fluctuations in your client load from week to week. If the idea of having your income bounce around sounds overbearingly stressful for you, then entrepreneurship via private practice might not be the answer. Or if you are only planning to see one or two clients a week. If you just want something super tiny. If you have an idea in mind that you just want to see one person on the side in addition to your job, it's not economically sound, and likely be a ton more work then you might have expected.

Those are things you should evaluate. With only one or two clients a week, on the side, part time, it would make it very difficult for you to cover your business expenses - unless by some miracle you own your own office already or you have an office for free. The math has to pencil for you. You should go into business to make money. To do that you need to charge more for your services than it costs you to pay for your office expenses, your salary, and your taxes otherwise the effort is not worth your time.

The Open Your Practice Blueprint and the accompanying Open Your Practice Master Course is designed for people who want to grow their practices and work in them full time, because that's where it makes the most sense. This guide is not for the dabbler. Let's go full time. Let's get you free. That's where the juice is worth the squeeze.

What do you think keeps people stuck in agency work?
Fear and confusion of intent. The first is fear. People that feel stuck in their job, feel a Grand Canyon leap worth of fear, and sometimes also confusion when the work is particularly rewarding for a moment. If you feel fear of the unknown, fear of the income shift, fear of not having an action plan, fear of not knowing how long it will take, or fear of failing, you are not alone!

If your inner monologue is saying, "What if I start it and it doesn't work? What if I start it and it's actually not what I want??" I was right there with you. I was afraid of all those things too.

I also remember times when my agency work made me feel good. Like when a client who was really working hard, really striving and fighting for their recovery. Or a family that made amazing leaps in how they related to each other, which completely changed the fabric of their family dynamic for the better.

The emotional lift I felt in these moments made it confusing and hard to leave my job. I also loved the people I worked with. They were amazing, dedicated people, who poured endlessly out of themselves for their clients.

I was also afraid of being isolated in private practice and not being able to consult with my colleagues on a regular basis about the tough stuff. You need to build a team around you so you don't feel like you are doing it alone. You need a trusted consult group. A community. People in your corner.

Lessons from Failure

What did you try initially to grow your private practice that didn't quite work?

In the beginning I didn't know what would work to bring me clients so I tried all sorts of things. Initially I volunteered for non-profit boards and assumed time commitments to try to generate clients and get my name out there. Those commitments ended up taking up a ton of time and not resulting in any client referrals. So when it was time to exit them, I did.

At the beginning I played a frustrating marketing game. I didn't really know how to market myself efficiently.

I also put my office in the wrong spot. I located my office in the downtown core of Seattle. At the time I believed that the central location was the best place for my office because it was in the center of several large businesses, and near a lot of people.

What ended up happening was in the peak hours that people wanted to come see me for therapy, from 3 - 6 pm, it was prime traffic time. I discovered that being downtown was actually prohibitive for my clients being able to come see me because of traffic. Eventually I moved my office to a location closer to my home that worked better for me and my clients.

When I had my downtown office I was often stuck in traffic as well. This forced me to limit the number of clients I could see in the evening so I could get home at a decent hour.

Another misstep was taking on clients during different parts of the day instead of batching them together in back-to-back sessions at times that were convenient for me. In almost desperation to fill my practice I took the attitude of, "Whenever you want to come in, that's totally fine." As a result, I had days that were really choppy and inefficient. I also ran into issues scheduling clients too close together and not having time to do notes between sessions.

Now I make sure that my sessions are exactly 53 minutes (minimum needed to bill for a full hour), which leaves 7 minutes for notes before the next client arrives for their session.

What advice do you have for new practitioners on scheduling?

Sit down with your calendar, planner, or practice management system. Determine which times work best for you to see clients. Determine which hours you want to be open. For example, if you want to see 25 clients per week, which 5 hour blocks will you schedule them in? Or this 8 hour block and this 3 hour block, etc. Don't just accept having clients show up whenever they can be there or what is best for them. They can and will make accommodations to come see you.

The core concept here is creating time-slots and then scheduling clients into those slots. This approach gives you the ability during your phone screen to say, "I have a 6 pm opening on Tuesday and a 3 pm on Friday. Which of those works better for you?"

What do you think causes stress and burnout in therapists?

The number one cause of burnout is poor self care. In this profession, regardless of credential: coaches, counselors, social workers, and therapists all give and give and give of themselves to everyone else. When you don't take time to take care of yourself you are running on an empty tank.

Another cause of burnout is trying to wear too many hats, trying to do too many jobs, or trying to do everything that is required in your business by yourself. This presents in cases where you feel like you have to be the CPA, you have to be your own consult group, you have to provide your own legal counsel, you process all of your own insurance claims for billing, you manage all of your own investments, and you are working on social media marketing to generate new clients.

You may be able to do all of the things that are required to run a small business over very short time periods but it is not sustainable over an extended period of time. You need to have time dedicated to intentional self care, and you need to understand that as a small business owner a lot is required of you. More is required of you in private practice than in a job because of the responsibilities that come with business ownership like taxes and paperwork.

How do you recover from difficult client sessions?

Consult group. You can do a certain amount of processing and put issues on a shelf in your mind until you can consult, because you won't have consult group every day. In extreme cases I reach out to my mentor to get advice on difficult moments that come up in therapy sessions. Work on giving yourself grace until you have the opportunity to speak with someone about the issue. Setting up outlets for stressful situations before issues arise is the best course of action.

There is a significant amount of stress and burnout associated with feeling responsible for others making changes in their lives. Remember that it is the client's responsibility to change, not yours. Changing others is not what we are here to do. We are here to help them look at their lives in a way that is different than they have in the past, and maybe create some pattern shift and help them achieve some insight, but the actual change must come from them.

Change is their responsibility. It is not your responsibility, nor can it be. We want to help so much. Especially when there isn't progress being made. We tend to take this on as our own failure.

Let's Get Personal

How do you set your goals?
I look at what I want to be doing at a particular moment in time, where I want to be, what I want life to look like, and I set those dreams as goals and then I work backwards from there.

You can't really know how to get there until you know what it is you want and where you are going.

If you identify the goal, say for example, "Two years from now I want to have a thriving private practice," let's work backwards from there. This is where I think our course comes in handy because we outline that for you. We work with you on identifying what you want life to look like and how you want to be feeling at a specific time in the future, and then you work backwards to get there.

How has life changed since becoming a mother?
As we sit here I have a child napping with a fever... It's shifted a lot of perspectives on what is important in life, and what I really want for our future as a family.

The timeline of how far into the future I look has drastically increased. I went from thinking about a 3-year plan to wondering what life would be like when our child is 18, almost two decades into the future.

You start to plan a little longer. You start to plan a little bigger. And do your best to stay grounded on what's important.

Do you have an effective morning routine that you can share?

I get coffee :) I like to get a slow start in the morning. I've never been that person that jumps out of bed and shouts, "Yes! The day has started!!" I'm a little more like grumpy cat in the morning.

Recently I started the habit of keeping a gratitude journal. I write down what I am grateful for in the day and the top 10 goals for my life that I am focused on. I write these out by hand every day. I've noticed it's made me a happier, more grateful person.

Why did you start Open Your Practice?

The lack of information on how to simply and efficiently start and run a private practice was agonizing to me. Not knowing what we are sharing with you here cost me a ton of money and it cost me a massive amount of time.

I became so incredibly frustrated with how inefficient it was to go from grad school with full licensure into private practice. I knew that it didn't have to be that way.

I knew that it would be hard work to build something but I wanted this information to be available for other people. I didn't want anyone else to have to struggle like I did. I think it's silly that here we all are wanting to help people and there's this huge Grand Canyon of a gap of missing information that's keeping us from doing that. It's beyond ridiculous.

I knew that if we built something that was efficient, made sense, and was affordable, that more people would make that leap and go into private practice. And thus more people would be helped.

When all of the baby-boomer therapists in private practice retire we are going to have a big-time drought in the field. And it's going to be really sad if people do not have access to resources as a result.

If you could invest \$5 and get \$100 back every year for the rest of your working lifetime, would you do it?
I think it's reasonable to take the perspective that you make investments upfront before you try and get something back. It's a helpful personality trait of someone who wants to go into private practice.

Nothing is without risk so you have to put a little bit out there to get the thing you want in the end. You have to make yourself a little vulnerable to get the thing that you want. And it's worth more when you do! If there was no risk in anything, and I just handed you something, would you place much value on it? I wonder if would I be as proud of myself, if I would value the experience as much, and be as enthusiastic about what I built? Probably not.

What else would someone need starting in private practice beyond the Open Your Practice Blueprint?
The Blueprint is great. It's concise, packed with value and tells you exactly what to do to open your private practice.

We go much deeper with the course that we built because we have more time to get into the nuances and the little details. For example, which phone solution is best? We give you our recommendation on that, and all the other tools that you need to select for your practice to cut down on the time.

We get really detailed about cash flow and how to setup your finances to where they benefit you the most. You come out the other side really feeling like this is not only possible, but you end up thinking, "Why wouldn't I do this?" Our live course attendees were overwhelmingly impressed with how clear we'd made this road to private practice.

Let's talk about the action items you will need to check off. The "what to do" checklist guide to open your practice. Let's go through this one by one so you understand what these items are, why they come in the order that they do, and then give some additional context behind them for the "what to do."

The Checklist to Open Your Practice

☐ **STEP 1:** OBTAIN YOUR PROFESSIONAL CREDENTIALS

The first order of business is to obtain your professional credentials: LMFT(A), LMHC(A), LICSW, CPC, HC, MCC, PhD., etc. If your professional credentials require licensure as they do in therapy, counseling and social work you will apply for your credentials through your state's governing body. For example, The Department of Health (DOH) in Washington state, or the BBS in California, and so on.

Each state and credential has specific requirements. Check with the governing body for up-to-date specifics on your credential. If your credential requires additional requirements beyond an initial license, you will need to complete those next.

☐ **STEP 2:** SATISFY SUPERVISION REQUIREMENTS, IDENTIFY AND HIRE A SUPERVISOR (IF APPLICABLE)

If you are going to work at an agency or take a job after graduation, and they offer supervision, then you can collect supervision hours through your workplace. If you are utilizing a group supervision option, make sure you are aware of the supervision requirements for your state.

Some states limit the number of people that can be in the room and still count it as a supervision hour. Make sure you regularly review the state laws pertaining to your credential.

Another option is individual supervision sessions. This option is actually my preference, even though it may cost more out of pocket for you upfront. I believe there is something really valuable about you being the only one in the room with your supervisor. There's more freedom to ask questions without feeling judged by your peers, and you may grow more as a clinician as a result.

☐ **STEP 3:** COMMIT TO OPEN PRIVATE PRACTICE

You've checked the boxes on your professional credentials. Your governing bodies have cleared you for launch. Are you ready to fly? Do you have a destination in mind? Private practice sounds nice this time of year.

You've hit that tipping point. Whether it's graduating from grad-school, or you are wanting the freedom that comes with private practice, you have to make a commitment to go for it. Trying to do this half way is not going to work. You need to be all in. Have you made your decision yet?

Consider defining a niche, or a specific population you want to serve. It's not a requirement to define a niche, but it can be very helpful if you do.

Laura's specialty came as a natural extension of the experience she gained working with eating disorders and families. So she was able to market herself as a specialist to people with needs in this area. Defining a niche or specialty can help you become known in your area by clinicians who refer out clients outside their specialty.

Ask yourself, "Who is my ideal client? What type of clinical work gets me fired up and is the most rewarding?" The eating disorder community in Seattle is small. Almost all of the providers in that specialty know each other. The same is true for clinicians that specialize in sex therapy. They all know each other, and can refer back and forth. A niche is not a requirement, you can be a generalist, but it is something to consider from the beginning once you've made the decision to go all in.

The next step is to add the first professional to your team, someone who can help you with 'the books.'

☐ **STEP 4:** IDENTIFY & HIRE A CPA

The amount of administrative paperwork required to run a therapy or coaching business is a shock to new practitioners. Keeping up with it is like having two full time jobs. You need a partner.

Identify and hire a CPA to advise and support your business. This is important because having a CPA is crucial in helping you understand your tax situation and track the cash flow for your business. Starting early with a CPA will benefit you the most.

Some of the steps you take on this list don't have to be in perfect linear order, but the reason you identify and hire a CPA early is so they can have a grasp on your start-up costs and you get them appropriately documented and factored into your tax picture. Your CPA can help you understand how to write off the business start up expenses from your taxes that you will incur as you get your business going.

Next, are you your business, or is your business a business? Let's talk about incorporation and limiting your personal liability through a business structure.

☐ **STEP 5:** INCORPORATE YOUR BUSINESS (PLLC)

Incorporated businesses offer more legal protection to their owners than those business owners that operate as a sole proprietor. (Check with your lawyer on this, we are explaining this for educational purposes, we are not giving you legal advice here.)

Incorporating is a crucial step in your journey to private practice and one we explain in detail in the Open Your Practice Master Course. There is a big difference between running your business as a PLLC (Personal Limited Liability Company), and a PC (Personal Company) or SP (Sole Proprietor).

First off, when owning a business where you will be conducting services with a license (such as a therapist, or a lawyer etc.) you need to have a PLLC versus an LLC. Incorporating your business as a PLLC limits your personal liability in a way that a PC and SP does not. You want to keep your personal assets safe from potential business liabilities, so incorporate as a PLLC.

☐ **STEP 6:** REGISTER/LICENSE YOUR BUSINESS WITH YOUR STATE'S DEPARTMENT OF REVENUE

Your professional credential is only one of the licenses you need to operate a business in private practice. You also need a business license from your state to operate, collect revenue, pay taxes, and operate business banking accounts.

Register your business with your state. Almost all states have online portals for you to complete this step in an hour or less.

If you don't register your business and obtain a business license you could be subject to fines and end up owing back taxes, fines, and penalties on all the revenue your business incurred since its inception. The CPA you hired (see step 4) can help you with this as well.

☐ **STEP 7:** REGISTER/LICENSE YOUR BUSINESS WITH YOUR CITY'S DEPARTMENT OF REVENUE

Many city governments have license requirements and tax obligations for businesses that operate within their boundaries.

Not all cities require licenses or that you collect and pay taxes to them directly, so check with your CPA and with the website of the city where you plan to practice for their department of revenue.

Save yourself a headache later, make sure you are in compliance from the beginning.

☐ **STEP 8:** SET UP BUSINESS BANK ACCOUNTS

Hey there business owner. You've got your licenses, now you need business bank accounts so you can collect payments from your clients and operate your business.

At a minimum you are going to want one business checking account and a business savings account.

In the Open Your Practice Master Course we walk you through how to structure a series of connected accounts to make cash flow management a breeze, and set you up with a structure so that you always have enough money for the things you need it for. Quarterly taxes for example... Good thing you have a CPA to help out.

The disaster scenario is to have all the money flow in, and you spend all of it because you haven't set up the cash flow properly. You need to have an account to set aside for estimated taxes (which are due quarterly), and so on. Ensure you are keeping this part of your business impeccably efficient and organized.

You will need some seed capital, or money that you use to pay for initial startup costs of your business. Transfer this money to your business account and use it as you spend on business expenses so that you keep your business expenses separate from your personal expenses, which is important come tax time.

Next you'll want to join your membership association which has some amazing benefits.

☐ **STEP 9:** JOIN MEMBERSHIP ASSOCIATIONS

Find and join the membership association that supports your credential. For example, AAMFT / AMHCA / NASW / AC.

Membership associations use their collective buying power to provide members with discounts on services such as malpractice insurance, access to current events in the field, and legal support. Most associations have an annual conference where you can network with others in your field to expand your professional network.

☐ **STEP 10:** PURCHASE MALPRACTICE INSURANCE

Malpractice lawsuits are a thing. You need protection against them in the form of a large insurance policy before you see clients.

Ensure that you purchase a policy with at least $1,000,000 single incident and $3,000,000 annual aggregate coverage.

You can purchase your malpractice insurance policy through your membership association, usually at a discount, or research a company on your own.

☐ **STEP 11:** REGISTER FOR YOUR NATIONAL PROVIDER IDENTIFICATION NUMBER (NPI)

If you ever plan to take insurance, then you need a National Provider Identification (NPI) number to identify yourself as a clinician. Your NPI is used by the insurance companies when submitting and processing claims for services provided.

You can register for your NPI number online. The purpose of the NPI system is to keep all the providers delivering care (such as doctors etc.) organized in a central database.

If you plan to take insurance, you must have an NPI number.

☐ **STEP 12:** SELECT OFFICE LOCATION

Where do you want to practice? You need a dedicated physical space to conduct therapy that provides confidentiality to your clients.

Selecting an office location is fairly straightforward, in theory. Yet it is one of the biggest areas we receive questions from our students on.

In the Master Course we discuss all the deeper level recommendations, but the high points are to pick a location that works for *your* life and for *your* schedule. Don't hesitate to keep looking until you find the space that feels right to you.

It's not enough just to pick out a space. You need a legal contract that ensures you have the dedicated right to operate your practice at that location for a defined term length.

☐ **STEP 13:** SIGN LEASE/SUBLEASE

Do not skip this step!! You must sign a legal, binding agreement that secures the space you plan to practice therapy.

Far too many clinicians have thought that they didn't need a lease because they were good friends with someone only to later find out that they were being evicted with less than 30 days notice. You don't want to have to uproot your entire practice in a fire sale, do you?

Make sure any agreement you enter into is legal and signed by all parties. Do NOT make handshake agreements with colleagues about the home for your business. A legal lease agreement brings clarity, and protects all parties involved.

☐ **STEP 14:** IF TAKING INSURANCE, BEGIN THE PANELING PROCESS WITH INSURANCE PROVIDERS

Paneling with insurance providers is the process of applying for and signing a contract to provide services at a defined rate to the beneficiaries of the respective insurance company.

That's a mouthful. And this can be one of the most time consuming parts of getting setup in private practice. Because of the lead time typically required, you should apply as soon as you have your office lease signed because an office address is required before you can begin the application process.

In the Master Course we dive deeply into the specifics; however, the basics to the insurance paneling process are:

- You can panel (aka: contract) with insurance companies individually
- If you want to work with multiple insurance companies you can save time by using a service to fill out a common application for multiple insurance companies
- Be prepared for a waiting game where patience and persistence are required

☐ **STEP 15:** CREATE OFFICE PAPERWORK/ LEGAL DOCUMENTS

Before you sign your first client you will need to purchase or create a set of new client paperwork. These documents make clear your professional relationship with your client and provide you protection in the case of legal action.

The forms and documents that you will be using on a regular basis for your practice include, but are not limited to:

- Biopsychosocial
- Disclosure statement (also known as a consent to treatment)
- Release of Information (ROI) form
- Privacy policy
- Services agreement
- Termination letter

☐ **STEP 16:** PURCHASE & SET UP A DIGITAL OFFICE MANAGEMENT SYSTEM

If you had to fill out a form one hundred times would you prefer to do it on paper with a pencil, or use a computer with copy and paste?

I trust you picked the computer. That is essentially the difference between trying to administer your practice by hand or using a digital office management system.

Having a digital office management system is probably the biggest workhorse of your private practice, and worth every penny that your service provider charges you monthly.

Practice management software handles scheduling, billing, charting, insurance claims, credit card transactions, email/messaging, some even offer tele-health options, *AND* it's all HIPAA compliant!

Remember that email in any form is not HIPAA compliant, and you must have a disclaimer about this in your email footnotes. If you want complete HIPAA compliant written communication with your clients: practice management software is for you.

Your time is money, and this type of software is the biggest time saver there is in private practice.

☐ **STEP 17:** PURCHASE PHONE/ VOICEMAIL SOLUTION

Your practice needs a phone and voicemail solution that is HIPAA compliant. It is your responsibility as a practitioner to ensure that you have the appropriate solutions in place.

Any voice over internet protocol (VOIP) service (Google Voice, for example) transmits data over the internet, and therefore is not HIPAA compliant.

There are several compliant options available. Because you are liable if it does not, you must verify in writing that the phone and voicemail solution you choose adheres to HIPAA regulations.

☐ **STEP 18:** DECIDE ON YOUR PRACTICE NICHE OR SPECIALTY

Hopefully you've been considering the specialty you plan to focus on for a while. Now is the time to make a decision, before you dive into crafting your marketing messaging.

Deciding to have a general practice (e.g. no specialty) is OK, though having a specialty will set you apart from other providers and make it easier for clients to find you.

You will need clarity on which niche, or segment of the market, you plan to focus on before you craft your promotional materials. This step has proven difficult to others so we have provided you with a few examples based on your specialty.

Mental Health Counseling
- Cognitive behavioral play therapy
- Substance abuse counseling
- Crisis counseling
- Behavioral counseling

- Trauma recovery counseling

Marriage & Family Therapy
- Couples therapy
- Family systems therapy
- Conflict and infidelity in marriage therapy
- Addiction and recovery in families therapy
- Trauma in relationships therapy

Social Work
- Mental health and substance abuse social work
- Child, family, and school social work
- Social work with military members and veterans
- Community social work
- Elderly care social work

Coaching
- Weight loss and body image coaching
- Health and wellness coaching
- Career & performance coaching
- Life coaching
- Transition & spiritual coaching

Once you have your niche or specialty identified you are ready to craft statements that make it easy for others to understand what you do and which clients are best for your practice.

☐ **STEP 19:** WRITE DESCRIPTION OF PRACTICE SERVICES & TAGLINE

You will need clear and concise language that describes who you are, what you do, who you help, and what benefit your clients receive when they work with you.

The reason this is important is that you need to be able to efficiently tell people about what you do and the clients you serve. It's a summary of your background, and what clients might expect to experience when they come to see you.

Your tagline, also known as a slogan, is a short phase that encapsulates the benefits your clients receive when they work with you, or a feeling they want, or something that is catchy for them to remember you by.

Here are a few examples:
- Find your balance
- Goodbye anxiety, hello peace
- Shaping the future of occupational therapy
- Return to being you
- You deserve to be heard
- For kids, play is therapy
- The path to your true potential

You will use your description of services copy and your tagline on your website, in your brochures, and anywhere you put your company in print. Having a written description of your practice services makes it easier for you capture the theme of your practice in a graphic image or logo for your business.

☐ **STEP 20:** DESIGN BRAND & PURCHASE PRACTICE LOGO

Think of all the top businesses. They all have brands & logos. All the top agencies? Yep, they all have brands and logos. Yet many practitioners miss this step. Can you picture the logo for Apple? If you hear

McDonald's do you know what they do by their brand?

Brands and logos create a feeling. They anchor your business in the consumer's mind and they make it much easier for people to remember you.

What do you want people to know you for? When someone says, "Hey, I'm looking for a great clinician that specializes in blank" ...your name comes to mind because you did a great job with your branding. That's the goal. Create something recognizable so that you are the first person who comes to mind.

There are many different ways to design a logo, and we are fans of it all. The takeaway here is that you need one for your practice. Once you have it you can put it on printed materials.

☐ **STEP 21:** DESIGN & PURCHASE BUSINESS CARDS

There's always a big debate about whether business cards are worth the money. Some say yes, some say no.

We say yes. Because they are so stinking cheap. You can get hundreds for around 10 bucks. And once you get them you need to give them all away as quickly as you can. (I think the people that say that business cards aren't worth the money kept them in a box- they only work when you give them out...)

People ask me for my business card all the time. If you don't have one, what will you leave with the person who asks you for a way to remember and contact you later? Do you think it is a good strategy to chance it to their short term memory?

I have run out of business cards before, and felt silly when I didn't have one to give out, because I knew that was a potential lost opportunity.

Should you hang all your marketing hopes on business cards alone? Of course not. Should you expect tons of referrals to come from them? Probably not. But you should have them because they are helpful and professional. Plus they remind people to visit your website.

☐ **STEP 22:** BUILD YOUR PRACTICE WEBSITE

The largest obstacle to your early success in private practice is that not enough people know who you are. Your challenge is obscurity. People are looking for what you do on the Internet and for that reason alone it is crucial that you have a website that lets them know you exist and tells them what you do.

There are so many options these days for easy website building. You certainly don't need to know how to write code in order to make a decent looking and professional site. All the website building platforms build the code for you. The modern programs for this make the technical part of website construction so easy.

Make sure that your website, logo, and business cards are branded together, with a common theme and feel to ensure that you have a professional presence on the Internet for your business.

The next step towards getting people online to know who you are and what you do, quickly, is partnering with large Internet traffic sources.

☐ **STEP 23:** REGISTER ON PSYCHOLOGY TODAY

For counselors, social workers, and therapists, the largest and most concentrated traffic source for people searching for your specialty is on Psychology Today.

Submit your application, and after your credentials are verified, you will be able to build your profile. Add your specialty, hours, insurance, contact information, and other details to your profile and you will begin to attract clients.

The membership comes at a cost but is worth every penny. They even provide you with some basic analytics, so you can see how your dollars are working for you.

In putting your website and Psychology Today profiles together you will have most of the ingredients you need to assemble your press kits.

☐ **STEP 24:** CREATE MARKETING PRESS KITS

Press kits are a more substantial, professional leave-behind than a stand-alone business card. Press kits are folders containing a collection of your printed marketing materials. This step on the checklist contains a bunch of mini-steps to assemble the components you will need.

Press kits typically include your business card, your practice brochure, a one-page bio/CV about yourself as a clinician/practitioner, pages of information about public talks you give, pages on articles, blog posts or books you've written, and other information that will help referral partners and potential clients who receive your press kit to learn about you, and more importantly know when and why to refer to you.

☐ **STEP 25:** VALIDATE BUSINESS LOCATION WITH GOOGLE PLACES

For decades now, Google has been the undisputed leader in online searches. Google controls the top 3 searched areas on the Internet: Google.com, YouTube.com, and maps.google.com (also known as Google Maps or Google Places).

Google is very interested in providing the most accurate and relevant results to their search customers, and this is especially true for businesses that have a physical location.

First, you will need to go through their setup wizard and verification process which confirms that you are able to receive mail at your office. Then you can construct a similar business profile for your business on Google Places (which feeds Google Maps) to what you built on Psychology Today.

☐ **STEP 26:** WRITE AND PRACTICE YOUR ELEVATOR PITCH & 30-SECOND NETWORKING COMMERCIAL

Quick. You have 10 seconds in an elevator to tell someone what you do. What do you say?

Often when you are out and about, and at every networking event, you will be asked, "So, what do you do?" You need a sharp and polished answer to this question when it comes up.

We recommend that you have a prepared response so that it rolls easily off the tongue. Two versions are best: a short 10-second elevator pitch, and a 30-second commercial when you have more time to engage in conversation.

Once you know what you are going to say, next you need to find venues to say it.

☐ **STEP 27:** FIND & JOIN NETWORKING VENUES

You might not be aware just how many networking venues are in your city or town right now. Most cities have a counselor's association, and many cities have several. Where Laura practices, the Seattle Counselors Association is the big one.

If you live near a major metropolitan area there are also likely groups for your specialty. IAEDP (International Association for Eating Disorder Professionals) for example, is one Laura frequented in the early days of her practice.

Visit several groups and find which ones resonate best with you. Become a member or one or two of them. Then go talk to people and tell them who you are and what you do!

☐ STEP 28: IDENTIFY CONSULT GROUP MEMBERS

Consult groups are made up of professionals that you can speak with about the issues that come up in your practice that do not violate your client's privacy or ethical obligations of confidentiality.

Choose people you trust. You want to be able to let yourself be vulnerable enough to talk about tough client moments, and ask questions in a space where you don't feel judged.

A big fear about going into private practice is feeling isolated. Having access to a consult group is a great way to make sure you are not feeling disconnected from your community, and that you are making ethical clinical decisions.

We recommend getting set up with a consult group as early as possible. If you are seeing clients you should also be seeing your consult group.

☐ STEP 29: PURCHASE OFFICE FURNITURE & DECOR

Time to design your space to do the work you love. When you lease a new office you typically get 4 walls, a door, and a window. It is up to you to design the look and feel of the interior space to suit your needs and make your clients feel comfortable.

This is such a fun part of the process! You get to decide how you want your space to look, and what configurations are going to work best for the types of clients you see.

Everyone has a creative side. Flex those muscles here, and create a space you feel great about when you walk through the door. Once you have the space designed to your liking you are just about ready for clients.

☐ **STEP 30:** GENERATE CLIENT REFERRALS THROUGH NETWORKING

To get clients you must talk about yourself. You must talk about yourself in a room full of people. You must introduce yourself to others, and talk about what you do. We know this thought may feel more than a little uncomfortable for you.

For those of you starting to hyperventilate, I totally get it. This is the hardest part of the job. Most therapists *hate* talking about themselves. We went into a field where we listen to others, and self disclosure is kept to a minimum!

It's not always natural or comfortable for us to do this step, but it's absolutely crucial. How do people know what you do or where to find you if you don't tell them? See step 27. Rinse and repeat.

☐ **STEP 31:** WRITE CLIENT SCREENING CHECKLIST & QUESTIONNAIRE

With a website, referral partners, and the word out about your practice you will start receiving phone calls from prospective clients. You need a screening checklist and a series of questions to guide the conversation and collect the information you need to determine if there is a good potential fit for you to start seeing them as a client.

What questions do you want to ask your clients before you see them? Most clients will have a list of questions before they come see you, and you can and should do the same. What if they are seeking a type of specific counseling you don't offer? It's important to know these things up front so you can refer out if needed.

Practice your phone screening skills with a colleague to refine your screening checklist and hone in on the most impactful questions you can ask on an initial call. Once this is in a good place you will use it every time your practice phone rings.

☐ **STEP 32:** USE SCREENING CHECKLIST TO SIGN NEW CLIENTS

Time to fill up your calendar. As you market and spread the word about your practice, your phone will continue to ring. Use the screening checklist you put together to conduct interviews and schedule initial client sessions with the prospective clients that meet your criteria.

Steps 32, 33, and 34 are concurrent and continuous throughout the life of your practice. You will sign new clients, serve them, administer your practice and focus on self care.

☐ **STEP 33:** SERVE CLIENTS & ADMINISTER YOUR PRACTICE

You've made it!!!!!!! Congratulations! You are seeing clients and are on your way to all those dreams you had outlined at the beginning. You've conquered fear, overcome hurdles, and persevered through the tough stuff!

This is the core business step which includes seeing clients at their scheduled time, charting, managing paperwork, billing, processing insurance, bookkeeping, and other administrative functions.

It's been quite a journey to get to this point! You should be exceptionally proud of yourself for getting here. Take time and reward yourself for this amazing achievement.

☐ **STEP 34:** PRACTICE REGULAR SELF CARE

This is likely THE most IMPORTANT step in the whole process!! Taking care of yourself will ensure that you continue to love what you do, and will reduce the risk of burnout.

If you practice good self care, you will ensure you have the time and space necessary to do quality work and manage your business effectively.

Check in and ask yourself how the business is going. How is your client load? Does it feel like too much, or could you add a billable hour or two a week? Are you seeing the clients you want to see? Do you have enough time for yourself?

When we take good care of ourselves as clinicians, our clients benefit directly. So does everyone else in our lives. Counseling is taxing work at any level of care, even private practice. So make sure you are still putting yourself first, and taking care of that big heart of yours.

Therapy Business Setup Checklist

- ☑ OBTAIN YOUR PROFESSIONAL CREDENTIALS
- ☑ SATISFY SUPERVISION REQUIREMENTS, IDENTIFY AND HIRE A SUPERVISOR (IF APPLICABLE)
- ☑ COMMIT TO OPEN PRIVATE PRACTICE & CONSIDER NICHE
- ☑ IDENTIFY & HIRE A CPA
- ☐ INCORPORATE YOUR BUSINESS (PLLC)
- ☐ REGISTER/LICENSE YOUR BUSINESS WITH YOUR STATE'S DEPARTMENT OF REVENUE
- ☐ REGISTER/LICENSE YOUR BUSINESS WITH YOUR CITY'S DEPARTMENT OF REVENUE
- ☐ SET UP BUSINESS BANK ACCOUNTS
- ☑ JOIN MEMBERSHIP ASSOCIATIONS
- ☑ PURCHASE MALPRACTICE INSURANCE
- ☑ REGISTER FOR YOUR NATIONAL PROVIDER IDENTIFICATION NUMBER
- ☒ SELECT OFFICE LOCATION *n/a*
- ☒ SIGN LEASE/SUBLEASE *n/a*
- ☒ BEGIN PANELING PROCESS WITH INSURANCE PROVIDERS *n/a*
- ☑ CREATE OFFICE PAPERWORK/ LEGAL DOCUMENTS
- ☑ PURCHASE PHONE/ VOICEMAIL SOLUTION
- ☑ DECIDE ON YOUR PRACTICE NICHE OR SPECIALTY

- [x] WRITE DESCRIPTION OF PRACTICE SERVICES & TAG LINE
- [x] DESIGN BRAND & PURCHASE PRACTICE LOGO
- [x] DESIGN & PURCHASE BUSINESS CARDS
- [x] BUILD YOUR PRACTICE WEBSITE *needs fine tuning*
- [ ] REGISTER ON PSYCHOLOGY TODAY
- [ ] CREATE MARKETING PRESS KITS
- [ ] VALIDATE BUSINESS LOCATION WITH GOOGLE PLACES
- [x] WRITE AND PRACTICE YOUR ELEVATOR PITCH & 30-SECOND NETWORKING COMMERCIAL
- [x] FIND & JOIN NETWORKING VENUES
- [x] IDENTIFY CONSULT GROUP MEMBERS
- [x] PURCHASE OFFICE FURNITURE & DECOR
- [x] GENERATE CLIENT REFERRALS THROUGH NETWORKING
- [x] WRITE CLIENT SCREENING CHECKLIST & QUESTIONNAIRE
- [ ] USE SCREENING CHECKLIST TO SIGN NEW CLIENTS
- [ ] SERVE CLIENTS & ADMINISTER YOUR PRACTICE
- [ ] PRACTICE REGULAR SELF CARE

Conclusion

Wow! That's a lot of stuff!! Can you imagine trying to figure out how to compile that list on your own!? We are so glad you no longer have to do that too.

This was such a labor of love, and something I am so proud to say we have put out into the world. If this helps even just one person streamline their start up and get going towards their dreams, it will have been totally worth it.

We are in the business of helping people. Obtaining the means to get to that end really shouldn't be as complicated as it has been in the past. I sincerely hope we have helped in the clarity department for you.

Be sure to let us know how you are doing! Your story is what this project is all about, so don't hesitate to share with us. Email us at info@openyourpractice.com, or connect with us on social media: Instagram: @openyourpractice, Facebook: Open Your Practice.

You can also join our exclusive Open Your Practice Community group on our facebook page! You'll have access to fellow group members, and exclusive Open Your Practice content. Don't forget to hashtag! #openyourpractice, #OYPcommunity.

See you soon!

Laura & Dustin Gransberry

This process won't be easy if you are second guessing yourself...

You may now have everything you need to open private practice. We've noticed that students fall into two types: those that want the what and those that want the how.

The what-to-doers want to know what to do and that's it. With a list of what to do they're off taking action, figuring out the challenge as they go. They're not bothered by ambiguity or making mistakes.

Grab pages 59 and 60 and check all the boxes. Then add one more: email us with your office address so we can send you an OYP office warming gift.

The how-to-doers, on the other hand, want to understand what they are doing, why they are doing it, how to do it, and what goes wrong if they don't do it right.

If this sounds like you, we recommend you take the Open Your Practice Master Course. Here is more about the course to determine if it is the right next step for you.

About The Open Your Practice Master Course

We started teaching the Open Your Practice Master Course in live events. It was a hit from day one. But there were three main areas we wanted to improve, to serve you better.

First, the live event required counselors, coaches, social workers, and therapists to travel to spend a weekend with us- which hopefully wasn't so bad- but because of the time constraint we had to move through the material quickly.

Second, we received feedback that more people in more locations wanted to attend and learn what we had to share than we could accommodate.

Third, people told us that they would prefer to have the material in the form of a home-study course so they could go through it at their own pace in the comfort of their homes at any time of day or night.

It took a lot of work to make that happen. In fact, it took over 3 years to complete all the research, test out the concepts, prove that every element in the formula works, and put it all together for you in an easy to follow, digestible, step-by-step format. But now we have something that we believe that you're really going to love.

This is not a quick fix, easy answer, or magic bullet that requires no work on your part to have a private practice. It's for people who are serious about learning what to do to make their dream a reality.

The Open Your Practice Master Course covers the business mindset you need to succeed as an entrepreneur; exactly how to setup a therapy business; how to find and setup your office; all the ins-and-outs of practice administration, how to keep yourself organized; how to structure a revenue plan for your practice, how to manage your cash flow, what to do about taxes, what you need to know about building a team around you; how to market your practice, how to attract the clients that you want; how to build a support network; all of the tools, technologies, and resources you need to gather to run your practice efficiently.

The material is delivered via a video series with a corresponding course-book which comes in a beautifully laid out 3-ring binder.

The course has everything you need to know and tells you what to do in the right order to open your private practice. And we cut out all the unnecessary fluff because we know your time is at a premium.

To request your copy write to us at info@openyourpractice.com, or visit www.openyourpractice.com

Acknowledgements

I want to thank a few people who helped this work come to fruition: First off, our editor (and my sister), Julia Mathews...who is still teaching me new things about language and grammar to this day. To my parents, for always supporting me in the very best way. And to Dustin: for his unwavering and steadfast belief that I can do absolutely anything. Without this solid foundation, I'm not sure where I'd be.

And finally, to our son: all we do is indeed truly just for you.

Notes

Notes